THE ORIGIN OF OUR UNIVERSE

DAVID A. BURNSIDE

ISBN 979-8-88751-330-0 (paperback)
ISBN 979-8-88751-331-7 (digital)

Christian Faith Publishing
832 Park Avenue
Meadville, PA 16335
www.christianfaithpublishing.com

Printed in the United States of America

The mystery of the origin of our universe has puzzled mankind for centuries. On one hand, theologians accept by faith that God created the cosmos. Faith is a strong belief in invisible principalities whose handiwork is visible. On the other hand, cosmology has provided hypotheses to explain how our universe came to be. Cosmology is the study of the universe, which provides scientific explanations to describe how preexisting conditions and natural laws bring life-forms into existence. The faith-versus-science controversy is founded on two belief systems: someone created the universe; and no one created the universe. Jastrow stated,

> For the scientist who has lived by
> his faith in the power of reason,
> the story ends like a bad dream.
> He scaled the mountains of igno-
> rance; he is about to conquer the

> highest peak; as he pulls himself
> over the final rock; he is greeted
> by a band of theologians who
> have been sitting there for centu-
> ries. (p. 116)

Has science proved our universe had a beginning and a beginner? What are the implications of our universe being created by a supreme intelligent designer? We will discuss the nineteenth century theories that are being challenged by twenty-first century discoveries to determine for ourselves if the evidence points to an intelligent designer.

The steady-state theory introduced the idea of an eternal universe that always existed and did not have a beginning. Albert Einstein published his general relativity theory in 1917. Jastrow (1978) pointed out that Einstein did not observe the implication of an expanding universe in his theory. Alexander Friedmann, a Russian mathematician, discovered Einstein's mathematical mistake, which suggested an expanding universe. In a letter to de Sitter, Einstein wrote, "The circumstance [of an expanding universe] irritates me," and in another letter about the expanding universe, "To admit such possibilities seems senseless." (Jastrow 1978, p. 28). Einstein's irritation propelled him to dismiss the emerging ideas of an expanding universe because an expanding universe implied the universe had a beginning. Einstein later added the "cosmological constant" to his original equation to solidify his idea that the universe was static. The idea of an expanding universe was gaining momentum in the scientific world. Edwin Hubble proved through theory and research that the universe is expanding. Hubble published his "Law of the Expanding Universe" around 1930. Later Einstein removed the "cosmological constant" from his equation calling it the biggest blunder of his career.

This newly accepted model of an expanding universe rocked the scientific community and ushered in new theories. The big bang theory explained the cosmos's beginning as a combustible mixture of cosmic gases exploding life into existence as we know it. The big bang and evolution has been widely accepted until recently. The intelligent design (ID) theory presents evidence that our universe is a result of intelligent thought. Some critics dismiss ID by stating it is a theory founded in religious beliefs. According to the Intelligent Design and Evolution Awareness Center (IDEA), "Intelligent design uses the scientific method to detect design." The following is a description of the scientific method:

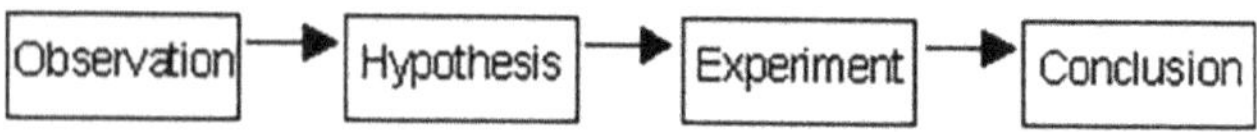

In contrast to the scientific methods applied to the big bang and intelligent design theories, the theological perspective is rooted in faith that God created the world as it is written in the Bible, "In the beginning God created the heavens and the earth." (Gen 1:1, King James Version). I am persuaded to accept by faith the theological perspective. Let us explore the additional scientific evidence (we've covered the expanding universe as the first line of evidence) that suggest our cosmos had a beginning, and then apply the laws of logic the following premise: "If the universe had a beginning, it must have had a beginner."

The second line of scientific evidence that suggest our universe had a beginning is thermodynamics—the study of energy. Energy exists in numerous forms such as heat, light, and electricity. Farabee (2010) teaches us that energy has a transforming nature and can convert from one form to another, but it cannot be created or destroyed. This is known as the first law of thermodynamics. Farabee (2010) expands his teaching into the second law of thermodynamics, stating, "In all energy exchanges, if no energy enters or leaves the system, the potential energy of the state will always be less than that of the initial state." If the universe had always existed, the diminishing energy would be more apparent from our perspective. Much like as we witness with a lawnmower in its initial state, full of gas (energy), eventually the lawnmower will die if the energy source is not replenished. These laws of thermodynamics imply that a source outside of space and time sustains the energy in our cosmos, because creating energy is outside of our capabilities.

Amo Penzias and Robert Wilson discovered cosmic microwave background and were awarded the Noble Peace Prize (NPP) in 1978. The radiation afterglow that Penzias and Wilson discovered while working for Bell Labs was in fact the evidence that pro—big bang believers theorized would be in existence if the theory were true. An article stored in the Bell Labs (1998) archives confirms the importance of this discovery:

> With their discovery of the cosmic microwave background in 1964, Arno Penzias and Robert Wilson placed the seal of

approval on the Big Bang Theory and shared the 1978 Nobel Prize in Physics for their discovery. Scientists consider the presence of cosmic microwave background to be proof that the universe was born at a definite moment, some 15 billion years ago.

Penzias and Wilson's discovery proved that the universe had a beginning.

Hubble's law of the expanding universe, the second law of thermodynamics, and Penzias and Wilson's cosmic microwave background discovery proves that our universe had a beginning. Let us go back to our premise: If the universe had a beginning, it must have had a beginner.

Based on our assumption, let us move forward into the cosmological argument. A cosmological argument is an argument intended to explain the existence of a first cause to everything in existence. This is to say a supreme intelligent designer (God) caused the cosmos to come into existence. The existence of the universe is undeniable because life exists and we can see the cosmos. Deductive reasoning applied to the cosmological argument suggests the following:

1. Everything that had a beginning had a cause.
2. The universe had a beginning (came into existence).
3. Therefore, the universe had a cause.

This model is known as the Kalam cosmological argument (KCA). The KCA was established by Muslim philosophers in the Middle Ages.

The idea that a supernatural being created the universe supports theological beliefs and challenges all thoughts and imaginations that attempted to exalt themselves above God. If twenty-first century science has proven beyond any reasonable doubt that our universe is the result of God's creation, the implications of this discovery will challenge personal worldviews and what is taught in our education system. A personal worldview is a set of truths, logical or illogical, embraced so deeply it becomes an individual's reality. This worldview affects how a person thinks, behaves, and feels. Individuals whose set of truths are contrary to an intelligent designer and His purpose for life will most likely seek alternatives to proven science or accept the fact that they were misled in their beliefs. Darwin's evolution theory will be revisited and scrutinized. If evolution is completely discredited, debates of how evolution is taught in our education system will receive more world interest.

Richard Dawkins and his followers will reevaluate the deeply rooted Darwinist views he expressed in his book *The God Delusion*. Dawkins (2006) wrote, "You cannot be both sane and well-educated and disbelieve in evolution. The evidence is so strong that any sane, educated person has got to believe in evolution." He is saying that if a person does not believe in evolution, he or she is insane or dumb. Lee Strobel (2004 student edition) clarified the definitions of evolution as:

> When some people talk about evolution, they mean merely that there has been change over time. If that is all there were to Darwinism, then there would not be any controversy, because everyone agrees there has been biological changes over time.
>
> Darwinism (updated as Neo-Darwinism) claims much more than that—it's the theory

that all living things are modified descendants of a common ancestor that lived long ago. According to Darwinism, every new species that has ever appeared can be explained by the result of natural selection acting on random genetic mutations. (p. 31)

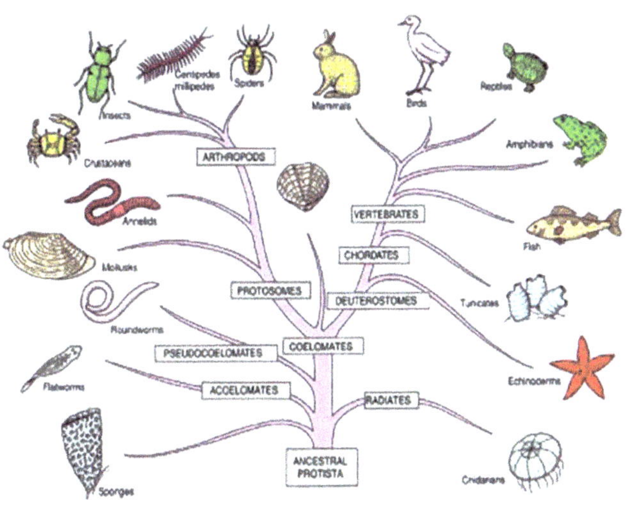

Evolution is based on the premise that our universe is infinite. In this infinite universe, an ancient simple organism that lived in the primordial ocean randomly mutated into all the life forms we see today. If modern science has proved that our universe is finite, evolution is discredited because it is based on a false premise. More than seven hundred reputable scientists have banded together and signed a short public statement, "The Scientific Dissent from Darwinism," expressing their skepticism about Darwin's evolution. The Discovery Institute (2001) article "The Scientific Dissent from Darwinism" states, "We are skeptical of claims for the ability of random mutation and natural selection to account for the complexity of life. Careful examination of the evidence for Darwinian theory should be encouraged." Darwin wrote in his *Origin of Species*, "If it could be demonstrated that any complex organ existed which could not possibly have been formed by numerous, successive, slight modifications, my theory would absolutely break down."

Michael Behe, a biochemist at Lehigh University, has demonstrated that complex organisms could not have been formed by numerous successive slight modifications. Behe (1996) has coined the term "irreducible complexity" from his discoveries in molecular biology and defined it this way: "By *irreducibly complex* I mean a single system composed of several well-matched, interacting parts that contribute to the basic function, wherein the removal of any one of the parts causes the system to effectively cease functioning." Irreducible complexity has been illustrated as a mouse trap consisting of five parts: hammer, spring, holding bar, catch, and platform. If one of those components were missing, the mouse trap would not function. From this illustration, we can see how the parts work together. The point is complex organisms operate as a system of parts; therefore, gradually mutating components of an organism would render it useless. Recent studies like this challenge the work of earlier researchers, who are convinced that life is a result of the theory of evolution.

The ideas of intelligent design and evolution are not compatible. The law of the noncontradiction helps us discover which one is false. This law states that opposite ideas cannot both be true at the same time and in the same sense. Further investigation into both ideas will eliminate one. Evolution does not explain the precision of our environmental conditions that make life possible on earth.

Earth's life-supporting conditions are our atmospheric makeup, our planet's axis tilt, our position in the Milky Way, gravity, and the complexity of man and woman. This precision or fine-tuning strongly points to an intelligent designer. Physics have provided the term "anthropic constant" to aid in our comprehension of our universe's fine-tuning that support life. An anthropic principle solidifies belief that life is not a result of natural selection or an accident. In section 5 of the In Plain Site website, an unknown author expresses, "The reality is that we live on an extremely rare planet perfectly positioned in an extremely rare solar system, ideally located in an extremely rare galaxy, within a highly improbable universe. Let us look at our rare Earth."

Our atmosphere is comprised of 21 percent oxygen, which makes life on Earth possible. If the composition of oxygen in our atmosphere were 15 percent, human beings would suffocate. Our planet is suspended on a twenty-three degree axis tilt which is perfect to sustain bearable surface temperatures. Temperatures on would be too extreme to sustain life if the axis tilt were slightly modified. The pinpoint precision of the earth's distance from the sun prevents our oceans from vaporizing or freezing. The oceans would vaporize if the planet were 1 percent closer to the sun, making life impossible. The force of gravity is positioned at exactly the right spot in the entire universe to support the existence of life. Strobel (2004) illustrated this phenomenon with an imaginary one-inch increment ruler that extends throughout the entire universe. Along this ruler, gravity is positioned on the inch mark relative to earth to support life. If gravity was positioned an inch to the left or an inch to the right, life would cease to exist. These facts are beyond my comprehension, so I can't lean on my own understanding to explain why things are the way they are. I'm struck with amazement and awe looking at details that life presents. If the universe is fine-tuned to support life, it was fine-tuned by the Most High God.

When I consider God as the creator of the universe, I'm in awe of His omniscience in creating space and time. To create space and time, God must exist outside space and time. Since space and time is finite, the Creator is infinite and eternal. God is omniscient, omnipotent, and omnipresent. A master in every field known to man: astrology, physics, biology, quantum physics, rocket science, anatomy, and the list goes on. The thought put into creation surpasses human understanding by leaps and bounds. The mystery of the origin of our cosmos might never be revealed to us until an appointed time only known by God. His greatest attribute is love because day after day He sustains creation with His power. The psalmist David eloquently wrote,

> The heavens declare the glory of God
> The skies proclaim the work of his hands
> Day after day they pour forth speech
> Night after night they display knowledge
> There is no speech or language where their voice is not heard
> Their voice goes out into all the Earth, their words to the end of the world. (Psalm 19:1–4, King James Version)

Psalms is a collection of hymns and poems spanning a thousand-year period (1400–400 BC) well before the noted advancements in science. I'm persuaded to believe God revealed this knowledge to David and us in order glorify the works of His hands.

BIBLIOGRAPHY

"1978 Nobel Prize in Physics." Nokia Bell Labs. Nokia Bell Labs. Accessed August 30, 2022. https://www.bell-labs.com/about/awards/1978-nobel-prize-physics/#gref.

Behe, Michael J. 1996. *Darwin's Black Box: The Biochemical Challenge to Evolution*. New York, New York: Free Press Publishing.

Brindle, Wayne A, and Carl J Diemer, eds. 1988. *The King James Study Bible: King James Version*. Nashville, Tennessee: Thomas Nelson.

Dawkins, Richard. 2006. *The God Delusion*. Boston, MA: Houghton Mifflin Co.

Discovery Institute. 2001. "A Scientific Dissent from Darwinism." Dissent from Darwin. Accessed August 30, 2022. http://www.dissentfromdarwin.org/about.php.

Farabee, M. J. 2010. "Laws of Thermodynamics." http://www.emc.maricopa.edu/faculty/farabee/ biobk/biobookener1.html.

"FAQ: Does Intelligent Design Theory Implement the Scientific Method?" IDEA Center. http:// www.ideacenter.org/contentmgr/showdetails. php/id/1154.

Geisler, Norman L., and Frank Turek. "Anthropic Principle: The Design Is in the Details." Accessed August 30, 2022. http://www.inplain-site.org/html/anthropic_principles.html.

Jastrow, R. 1978. *God and the Astronomers*. New York, NY: Norton Publishing.

Strobel, L. 2004. *The Case for a Creator*. Grand Rapids, Michigan: Zondervan.

————. 2004. *The Case for a Creator Student Edition*. Grand Rapids, Michigan: Zondervan.

TalkOrigins Archives. n.d. "Irreducible Complexity and Michael Behe, Do Biochemical Machines Show Intelligent Design?" http://www.talkori-gins.org/faqs/behe.html.